AF260866

This book that encourages spiritual growth and a realtionship with God belongs to:

God Says I'm Enough,
So I'm Going to
Relax In Him
Yolanda Lance, BA, M.ED, ED.S,
Jah'NaY and Jae'Dyn McDowell

ISBN: 978-1-972454-05-3
God Says I'm Enough, So I'm Going to Relax In Him

Yolanda Lance, Jah'Nay McDowell or Jae'Dyn McDowell
Conyers, GA
www.yolandipity.net
yolandipity@gmail.com or yolandaeducates@yahoo.com

All scriptures used are referenced from the King James Version of the Bible.
Printed in the United States of America

About the author

Yolanda, owner of Yolandipity LLC, is a faith-filled writer and encourager with a heart for helping women grow spiritually and discover their identity through the Word of God. With a background in psychology, education, and social services, she brings wisdom, warmth, and biblical truth to every page. Passionate about guiding others toward a deeper relationship with God, Yolanda creates resources that speak to the soul, reminding women that they are seen, known, and loved by their Creator.

Originally from vibrant Miami, Florida, and now rooted in the peaceful surroundings of Georgia, Yolanda finds inspiration in God's creation, quiet moments, and the strength of sisterhood. She is a devoted mother, joyful grandmother, and a woman who treasures faith, family, and community.

This journal is dedicated to every woman who's ever doubted her worth, second-guessed her voice, or shrunk herself to make others comfortable.

This journal is for you!
May these 30 days of truth remind you that you don't have to hustle for validation when Heaven already calls you chosen, beloved, and enough.
To the daughters of the Most High, the late bloomers, the bold dreamers, and the quiet warriors, you are blossoming boldly, beautifully, and biblically, and the world is better because of it.

And to the 30 fierce and faithful women in the Bible, thank you for paving the way with your stories, your strength, and your surrender.
We're taking notes and taking names.
Now sis… exhale. God says **you're** enough.
So y'all can relax.

**With love & holy sass,
Yolanda, Jah'Nay, and Jae'Dyn**

Can represent...

Age of Readiness for Ministry or Leadership:

Jesus began His public ministry at age 30 (Luke 3:23). Levites began their priestly duties at age 30 (Numbers 4:3). Joseph became second in command of Egypt at age 30 (Genesis 41:46). **These examples point to 30 as the age of spiritual and personal maturity, when one is considered ready to carry significant responsibilities.

Time of Mourning or Transition

Mourning for Moses lasted 30 days (Deuteronomy 34:8). **This suggests 30 can represent a transition or preparation period, especially after loss or before entering a new phase of life.

Betrayal and Redemption

Judas betrayed Jesus for 30 pieces of silver (Matthew 26:15). This fulfilled the prophecy in Zechariah 11:12-13, where 30 pieces of silver was considered the price of a slave, symbolizing how the Messiah would be undervalued. Here, 30 represents a painful cost, both literal and symbolic, of rejection and betrayal, but also sets the stage for ultimate **redemption** through Jesus.

Table of "I Am" (contents)

Table of "I Am" (contents)

TRACK YOU PROGRESS

1. Journal entry #1 completed ______
2. Journal entry #2 completed ______
3. Journal entry #3 completed ______
4. Journal entry #4 completed ______
5. Journal entry #5 completed ______
6. Journal entry #6 completed ______
7. Journal entry #7 completed ______
8. Journal entry #8 completed ______
9. Journal entry #9 completed ______
10. Journal entry #10 completed ______
11. Journal entry #11 completed ______
12. Journal entry #12 completed ______
13. Journal entry #13 completed ______
14. Journal entry #14 completed ______
15. Journal entry #15 completed ______

Are you Ready?

LET'S GO!

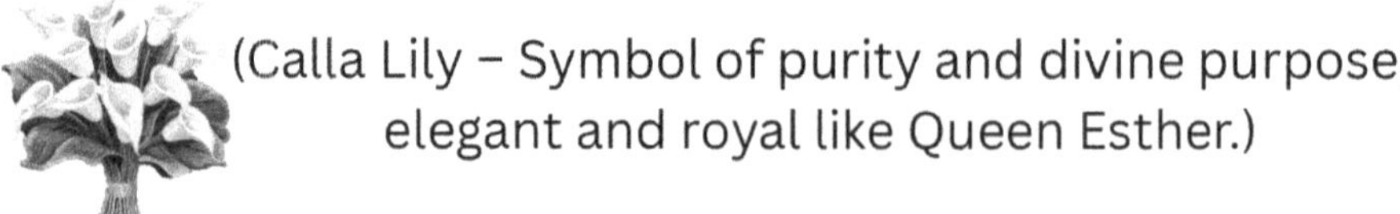

(Calla Lily – Symbol of purity and divine purpose;
elegant and royal like Queen Esther.)

"I Am" chosen for a purpose, like Esther. Esther 4:14 – "For such a time as this…"

Esther was a young Jewish woman living in Persia during a time when her people faced great danger. After being chosen as queen, she hid her true identity as a Jew until a crisis forced her to take a stand. When a royal official named Haman plotted to destroy the Jewish people, Esther's cousin Mordecai urged her to speak to the king and plead for their lives. This was a dangerous request.

In those days, approaching the king without being summoned could result in death. But Mordecai's words reminded Esther that her royal position wasn't by chance. He said, "Who knows but that you have come to your royal position for such a time as this?" (Esther 4:14). Esther realized that she had been chosen by God for a greater purpose, to save her people.

With courage and faith, Esther stepped forward. She prayed, fasted, and then bravely approached the king. God used her obedience to change the course of history. Her story shows us that even when we feel unsure or afraid, God places us in specific situations for a reason.

Like Esther, we are not where we are by accident. God can use each of us, our talents, voices, and choices, to carry out His greater plan. When we say, "I am chosen for a purpose," we recognize that our lives have meaning beyond ourselves. We may be here for such a time as this.

Reflective Questions

Do you believe that God has placed you where you are "for such a time as this"? ______________________________________
What purpose might He be calling you to step into right now, even if it feels risky or uncertain? ____________________________
____
What fears or doubts might be holding you back from fully embracing the role God has chosen for you? ___________________
____
How can you cultivate courage and trust like Esther to fulfill God's plan for your life? _________________________________
____
____

Today's affirmation: "I Am chosen for a purpose."

Prayer Prompt

Heavenly Father, thank You for choosing me and placing me where I am for a purpose. Just like Esther, I want to be bold and obedient, even when I feel unsure or unqualified. Help me to recognize the opportunities You've placed before me "for such a time as this." Give me the courage to say yes to Your calling and to trust that You are with me every step of the way. Today, I ask You to show me...

____
____
____
____
____
____

 (White Rose – Represents purity, faith, and devotion.)

"I Am" strong in my faith, like Mary, mother of Jesus. Luke 1:38 – "I am the Lord's servant…"

Mary was a young woman living in Nazareth when her life changed forever. One day, the angel Gabriel appeared to her with an astonishing message: she would give birth to the Son of God. Though Mary was a virgin and not yet married, the angel assured her that this child would be conceived by the Holy Spirit and that He would be the Savior of the world.

In that moment, Mary had every reason to be afraid. She could have been rejected by Joseph, her family, and her community. She didn't know all the details of how things would unfold, but she knew the One who had called her. Instead of responding with fear or doubt, Mary answered with faith: "I am the Lord's servant… May your word to me be fulfilled."

This simple yet powerful response revealed Mary's deep trust in God. She didn't need to have all the answers; she simply believed that God's plan was good, and she was willing to be part of it. Her faith wasn't passive—it was strong, active, and courageous. Mary carried the Son of God, raised Him, and stood by Him throughout His life, even at the foot of the cross.

Mary's story reminds us that true faith means saying "yes" to God, even when it's hard and you feel uncertain. Being strong in faith doesn't mean we never feel fear, it means we trust God more than our fear. Like Mary, we can say: "I am the Lord's servant."

Reflective Questions

Like Mary, are you willing to surrender your plans and say, "I am the Lord's servant," even when you don't understand what God is doing? ____
What area of your life needs deeper trust and surrender to God?

____

____

How can you strengthen your faith to respond with obedience and humility when God calls you to something unexpected or difficult? ____

____

What does saying "yes" to God look like for you today?

____

____

Today's affirmation: "I Am strong in my faith."

Prayer Prompt:

Lord, I want to be like Mary, full of faith and willing to trust You, even when I don't fully understand Your plan. Help me to say, "I am the Lord's servant," with a surrendered heart. Strengthen my faith so I can walk in obedience, humility, and courage. Teach me to listen for Your voice and respond with a confident "YES!" Today, I surrender my will and my plans to Yours. Help me to respond to you with faith and trust. The parts of your plan for my life that I am willing and learning to trust You are...

____

____

____

____

____

____

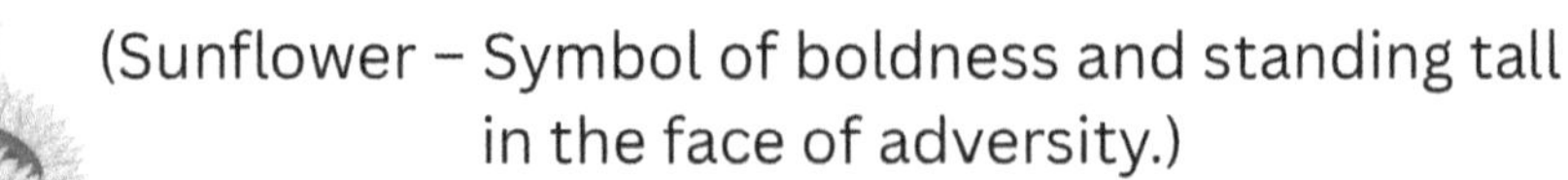

"I Am" courageous in the face of fear, like Deborah. Judges 4:9 – "I will surely go with you."

Deborah was a prophetess and judge in Israel during a time when the people were oppressed by a powerful enemy. While many were afraid, Deborah stood out as a strong and faithful leader who listened to God's voice. She used her position not just to settle disputes but to guide the nation with wisdom and boldness.

When God instructed Deborah to send Barak, a military commander, into battle against Sisera, the ruthless commander of the enemy's army, Barak hesitated. He was so unsure, he told Deborah he wouldn't go unless she went with him. Without hesitation, Deborah replied, "I will surely go with you." Her response was not just about presence—it was about courage. She was willing to go into danger because she trusted God completely.

Deborah's bravery inspired others. Because she was willing to act in faith, God brought victory to Israel. She didn't let fear control her. Instead, she faced uncertainty with confidence, knowing that the Lord was leading the way.

Deborah's story teaches us that courage doesn't mean we're never afraid; it means we move forward anyway, trusting God's power more than our own. Like Deborah, we can choose faith over fear. We can say, "I am courageous in the face of fear," because we know God goes before us.

When fear or uncertainty rises, do you lead with faith and courage like Deborah, or do you wait for others to go first? ______________

What would it look like to trust God more boldly in this season of your life?

How is God calling you to rise up and lead, whether in your home, workplace, or community? ________________________________

How how can you depend on His strength, not your own, to move forward with confidence? ________________________________

Today's affirmation: "I Am courageous in the face of fear."

Prayer Prompt:

God, when fear tries to silence me or make me shrink back, remind me of Deborah's courage. Fill me with boldness to go where You lead, speak when You call, and stand firm when others hesitate. Help me to trust that You are with me and that I don't face challenges alone. Help me to be brave and step out in faith. Today, I choose to move forward in faith. Lord, give me courage to...

"I Am" loyal and loving, like Ruth.
Ruth 1:16 – "Where you go, I will go…"

Ruth was a woman of great love, loyalty, and faith. After the death of her husband, she faced a crossroads: return to her own people in Moab or stay with her mother-in-law, Naomi, and follow her to a new and uncertain future in Israel. Most people would have chosen the easier, most comfortable path, but Ruth's heart was full of compassion and commitment.

With powerful words, Ruth declared to Naomi, "Where you go, I will go…" Her loyalty wasn't just about staying with family; it was a reflection of her deep love, not only for Naomi, but for Naomi's God. Ruth left behind her homeland, her culture, and her comfort to step into the unknown out of love and faith.

Ruth's actions didn't go unnoticed. In time, she found favor in Israel, met and married a kind man named Boaz, and became the great-grandmother of King David—and part of the family line of Jesus.

Her story teaches us that love and loyalty are powerful virtues. They shape lives, build trust, and honor God. Ruth's devotion shows that true love isn't just words, it's sacrifice, commitment, and choosing others even when it's hard.

Like Ruth, we can be known for our faithful hearts. When we say, "I am loyal and loving," we reflect God's character to the world.

In what relationships or circumstances is God calling you to show loyalty, love, and selflessness, even when it's hard or uncertain?

____

____

How can you reflect Ruth's faithfulness in your own life?

____

____

Are you willing to trust God enough to follow Him into the unknown, like Ruth did with Naomi? ________________________
What might you need to leave behind to fully walk in obedience and love? ____________________________________

____

____

Today's affirmation: "I Am loyal and loving."

Prayer Prompt:

Lord, give me a heart like Ruth's, loyal, loving, and faithful. Teach me to show steadfast love in my relationships, to stand by others with grace and strength, and to follow You wherever You lead. Help me to love with commitment, not convenience, and to trust You even when the path ahead is unfamiliar. Help me to be obedient to who you are calling me to love and walk alongside. Help me to show faithfulness and trust in this current season in my life. Today, I ask You to help me be loyal in...

____

____

____

____

____

 (Tulip – Symbol of answered prayer and deep, sincere love.)

"I Am" heard by God, like Hannah.
1 Samuel 1:27 – "I prayed for this child,
and the Lord granted me…"

Hannah was a woman who longed to have a child. Year after year, she waited, prayed, and cried out to God with a heart full of hope and sorrow. Others around her didn't understand her pain. Some even made fun of her. But Hannah never gave up on God. Instead of letting her heart become bitter, she brought her burden before the Lord in prayer.

One day, she went to the temple and poured out her soul, weeping as she prayed silently. She made a promise to God: if He gave her a son, she would dedicate him back to Him for His service. God saw her tears. He heard her prayer. And in time, Hannah gave birth to a son...Samuel, who would grow up to be a great prophet and leader of Israel.

When her prayer was answered, Hannah didn't forget her promise. She returned to the temple with Samuel and said, "I prayed for this child, and the Lord granted me what I asked of Him." Her story is a beautiful reminder that God listens. He hears not just the words we say, but the cries of our hearts.

Hannah's faith teaches us that no prayer is too small or too silent for God to hear. When we feel overlooked or forgotten, we can remember her story and say with confidence, "I am heard by God."

Reflective Questions

Do you trust that God hears your prayers, even when the answers take time? ____

How can you remain faithful and honest in prayer like Hannah, especially in seasons when you want something from God?

____

____

What have you prayed for with deep hope or tears? ____________

____

How can you offer those desires to God again today, with open hands and a heart full of faith? ____________________________

____

____

Today's affirmation: "I Am heard by God."

Prayer Prompt:

Lord, thank You for being a God who hears my prayers. Just like You heard Hannah's cry, I trust that You listen to the deepest desires of my heart. Even when I don't see answers right away, help me remain faithful, hopeful, and honest before You. Help me to trust You wholeheartedly.   Strengthen my faith in the waiting period, and remind me that You are always working. Today, I bring before You...

____

____

____

____

____

____

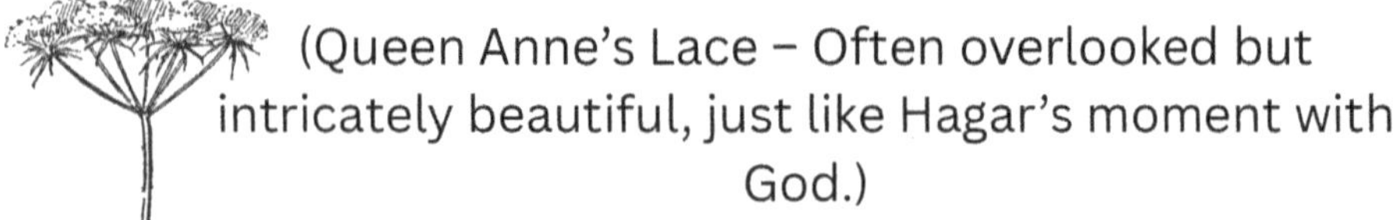

"I Am" seen and valued, like Hagar.
Genesis 16:13 – "You are the God who sees me."

Hagar's story is one of pain, struggle, and ultimately, hope. She was a servant in the household of Abraham and Sarah, and her life was not easy. When Sarah became impatient waiting for God's promise of a child, she gave Hagar to Abraham as a surrogate. Hagar became pregnant, but instead of being celebrated, she was mistreated and pushed aside.

Feeling unwanted and alone, Hagar ran away into the wilderness. It was there, far from anyone else, that God met her. An angel of the Lord appeared to her and spoke words of hope, reassurance, and promise. In that sacred moment, Hagar gave God a name: El Roi, which means "The God who sees me." She was the first person in the Bible to name God in such a personal way.

Hagar's story reminds us that even when we feel invisible, cast aside, or alone, God sees us. He knows our pain, our circumstances, and our worth. He values us not for our status or what others say about us, but because we belong to Him. To say, "I am seen and valued, like Hagar," is to declare that our worth doesn't come from people; it comes from God. And He is the God who sees us clearly, loves us deeply, and never looks away.

Reflective Questions

Do you truly believe that God sees you, your struggles, your pain, and your worth, even when you feel overlooked or alone? ________
____

How does knowing that God sees you change the way you see yourself? ____
____
____

Like Hagar, how can you respond to God's loving attention in your life? ____
____

What would it look like to live each day knowing that you are fully seen, known, and valued by God? ______________________
____
____

Today's affirmation: "I Am seen and valued by God."

Prayer Prompt:

Lord, thank You for being the God who sees me fully, deeply, and compassionately. Like Hagar, I've had moments of feeling unseen, forgotten, or overlooked. But You know my name, my story, and my heart. Remind me today that I am not invisible to You. Help me to walk in the confidence that I am seen, known, and deeply valued. Help me to bring to You all of my emotions, struggles, and victories. Today, I choose to trust You with...

____
____
____
____
____
____

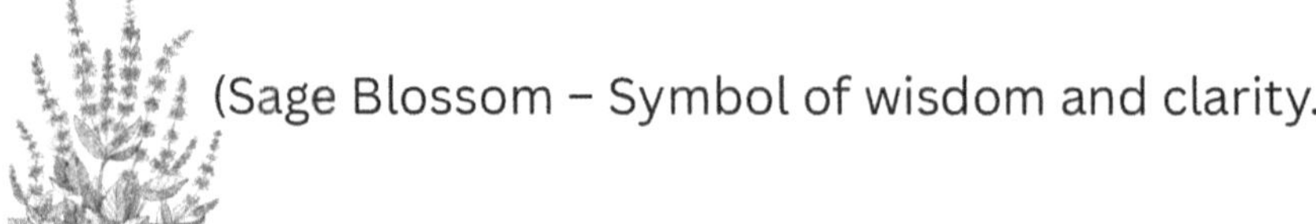
(Sage Blossom – Symbol of wisdom and clarity.)

"I Am" wise and discerning, like Abigail.
1 Samuel 25:33 – "Blessed is your discernment..."

Abigail was a woman known for her wisdom, grace, and courage. She was married to a wealthy but foolish man named Nabal, who insulted David, the future king of Israel, when David asked for food and kindness after protecting Nabal's shepherds in the wilderness. Nabal's harsh response offended David, and he set out with his men to take revenge.

When Abigail heard what had happened, she quickly and wisely stepped in. Without waiting for her husband's permission, she gathered gifts, met David on the road, and humbly spoke to him with great wisdom and discernment. She reminded David of God's promises and urged him not to act in anger or shed innocent blood.

David was moved by Abigail's words. He praised her and said, "Blessed is your discernment." Because of her courage and insight, she stopped a disaster and brought peace. Later, after Nabal died, David honored Abigail's character by making her his wife.

Abigail's story teaches us that wisdom isn't just about knowledge; it's about knowing when and how to act in ways that honor God and bring peace. She didn't allow fear or pride to lead her decisions. Instead, she used discernment, humility, and faith to speak truth and protect others.

When we say, "I am wise and discerning, like Abigail," we affirm that with God's guidance, we too can speak with clarity, act with courage, and bring peace to difficult situations.

Reflective Questions

In challenging or tense situations, do you pause to seek God's wisdom before you speak or act, like Abigail did? ________________ How can you grow in discernment and grace under pressure?

____

____

What decisions are you facing right now that require Godly wisdom? ____

____

How can you invite the Holy Spirit to guide your thoughts, words, and actions with clarity and peace? ___________________________

____

____

Today's affirmation: "I Am wise and discerning."

Prayer Prompt:

Lord, thank You for the gift of wisdom and discernment. Like Abigail, help me to respond with grace, courage, and clarity in difficult situations. Teach me to pause, seek Your guidance, and act in a way that honors You and brings peace. When emotions run high or decisions are unclear, help me to hear Your voice above all else. Today, I ask for wisdom in...

____

____

____

____

____

____

____

 (Peony – Represents joy, celebration, and abundance.)

"I Am" joyful in God's promises, like Elizabeth. Luke 1:25 – "The Lord has done this for me."

Elizabeth was a righteous and faithful woman who served God alongside her husband, Zechariah. Though they were both devoted to the Lord, they lived with deep disappointment: they had no children, and they were well past childbearing age. In their culture, this brought shame and sorrow, but Elizabeth never stopped trusting in God.

One day, the angel Gabriel appeared to Zechariah with stunning news: Elizabeth would have a son. This child would grow up to prepare the way for the Messiah. That promise was fulfilled when Elizabeth became pregnant with John the Baptist. Her long-awaited blessing brought overwhelming joy, not only because her shame was lifted, but because it showed that God's timing and promises are always trustworthy.

When Elizabeth felt her miracle growing inside her, she exclaimed, "The Lord has done this for me." Her joy wasn't just about having a child; it was rooted in the faithfulness of God. She saw her blessing as a sign of God's love and His ability to do the impossible.

Elizabeth's story reminds us that God hears the longings of our hearts. Even when answers seem delayed, His promises never fail. Joy comes not just from receiving what we hope for, but from knowing that God sees us, remembers us, and fulfills His Word. When we say, "I am joyful in God's promises, like Elizabeth," we are choosing to celebrate God's faithfulness, whether we're still waiting or already holding the answer in our hands.

Reflective Questions

Do you take the time to recognize and celebrate the ways God is working in your life, even in quiet or long-awaited seasons? ______ What has the Lord done for you that you can rejoice in today?

How can you remain joyful and hopeful in God's promises, even when you don't yet see the results? ____________________________

What helps you stay rooted in faith like Elizabeth did? __________

Today's affirmation: "I Am joyful in God's promises."

Prayer Prompt:

Gracious God, thank You for being faithful to Your promises. Like Elizabeth, I want to live with joy and gratitude for all You have done in my life. Even in seasons of waiting or silence, help me to trust that You are working behind the scenes. Fill my heart with joy, not just in what You've done, but in who You are. Today, I praise You for... ____________________________________

I am joyfully expecting and thanking You today for? __________

(Red Tulip – Represents passionate purpose
and bold love.)

"I Am" filled with purpose, like Mary Magdalene.
John 20:18 – "I have seen the Lord!"

Mary Magdalene was a faithful follower of Jesus whose life was completely transformed by His love. The Bible tells us that Jesus healed her by casting out seven demons (Luke 8:2). After this miracle, Mary became one of His most devoted supporters. She followed Him closely, supported His ministry, and stayed near Him even when others walked away.

When Jesus was crucified, Mary Magdalene remained by His side, witnessing His suffering and death. While many hid in fear, Mary stood at the cross. And early on the third day, she went to the tomb, hoping to care for His body. Instead, she found the tomb empty, and became the first person to see the risen Christ.

In one powerful moment, Jesus simply said her name: "Mary." At once, she recognized Him. Her sorrow turned to overwhelming joy. Jesus then gave her an important mission; she was the first to announce His resurrection to the disciples. In doing so, Mary Magdalene became known as the very first witness to the good news of Easter.

Mary's story reminds us that Jesus values our devotion, sees our faithfulness, and entrusts important work to those who love Him deeply. She was not a background follower, she was front and center at the resurrection because of her unwavering love and loyalty. When we say, "I am devoted to Jesus, like Mary Magdalene," we claim the same heart of deep love, faithfulness, and courage to follow Him, no matter what.

Reflective Questions

Like Mary Magdalene, are you living with a clear sense of purpose rooted in your relationship with Jesus? ______________________

How are you using your voice and life to declare, "I have seen and know the Lord"? ______________________________

____

____

What distractions, doubts, or past experiences might be clouding your sense of purpose? ____________________________

____

How can you refocus your heart to walk boldly in the calling God has given you? __________________________________

____

____

Today's affirmation: "I Am filled with purpose."

Prayer Prompt:

Lord, thank You for calling me by name and filling my life with purpose. Like Mary Magdalene, I want to live as a bold witness of Your love and power. Help me to recognize the unique mission You've given me and to walk in it with joy and confidence. Let my life declare, "I have seen and know the Lord!" in both word and action. Help me to reflect Your presence to others. Today, I offer myself to You and ask for direction with...

____

____

____

____

____

____

____

(Cactus Flower – Grows in harsh conditions, blooming with resilience.)

"I Am" brave in adversity, like Jael.
Judges 4:21 – She took action when others hesitated.

Jael is one of the most unexpected heroines in the Bible. Her story appears during a time of war and oppression, when Israel was under attack by the Canaanite army led by a cruel commander named Sisera. While Israel's general, Barak, and the prophetess Deborah led the charge in battle, it was Jael, a seemingly ordinary woman, who delivered the final blow that brought victory.

After fleeing the battlefield, Sisera sought safety in Jael's tent. She welcomed him in, gave him milk, and let him rest, seeming to offer peace. But Jael knew the danger he posed to her people. In a bold and courageous move, she acted when no one else could. While Sisera slept, she took a tent peg and hammer, tools she likely used every day, and ended the threat he posed.

Jael didn't wear armor or carry a sword. She wasn't a soldier or a prophet. But she used what she had, right where she was, and stepped up with quiet bravery in a moment of great adversity. Her courageous act changed the course of the battle and led to peace in Israel.

Jael's story reminds us that bravery doesn't always look like standing on a stage or leading a crowd. Sometimes it looks like acting wisely and boldly behind the scenes. Being brave in adversity means choosing to do what is right, even when it's hard or risky. When we say, "I am brave in adversity, like Jael," we claim the courage to act when God calls us, trusting that He can use even the ordinary to accomplish the extraordinary.

Reflective Questions

When you face adversity or difficult decisions, do you shrink back in fear or rise with courage and conviction like Jael? ____________ What helps you move forward when others hesitate? __________

____

____

What "tent peg" (strength, gift, opportunity, etc.) has God placed in your hands right now, and how can you use it bravely to stand for what is right, even when it's uncomfortable or risky? ________

____

____

What are the challenges that you are facing right now that require you to act with courage? ___________________________________

____

____

Today's affirmation: "I Am brave in adversity."

Prayer Prompt:

Lord, give me the courage to act when You call me, especially in moments of adversity. Like Jael, help me to recognize divine opportunities, even when they come in unexpected or challenging ways. Strengthen me to move forward in faith when others hesitate, trusting that You have equipped me for such a time. Today, I ask for bravery to...

____

____

____

____

____

____

____

(Forget-Me-Not – Symbol of patient faith
and remembrance of promises.)

"I Am" faithful in waiting, like Sarah.
Genesis 21:1–2 – God fulfilled His promise.

Genesis 21:1–2 – "The Lord was gracious to Sarah as he had said, and the Lord did for Sarah what he had promised. Sarah became pregnant and bore a son to Abraham in his old age…" Sarah's story is a powerful example of faithfulness and patience. For many years, Sarah and her husband Abraham longed for a child, but the promise seemed impossible. Sarah was well past the age of childbearing, and it seemed like God's promise might never come true. Despite her doubts and moments of struggle, Sarah continued to trust God's timing.

After waiting for many years, God finally fulfilled His promise. Sarah gave birth to Isaac, a miracle baby born in her old age. This joyful moment was the result of years of faithfulness and hope, even when the answer seemed delayed.

Sarah's life reminds us that God's promises are always worth waiting for. Faithfulness in waiting means holding onto hope, trusting God's plan, and believing that His timing is perfect, even when we don't understand the delay.

When we say, "I am faithful in waiting, like Sarah," we declare our trust in God's promises, knowing that He is always working for our good—even in the waiting.

Reflective Questions

How do you respond in seasons of waiting, do you trust God's timing, or do you struggle with doubt and impatience? _________

____

What can you learn from Sarah's journey of faith? _____________

____

____

What promise or prayer are you still holding onto? _____________

____

How can you remain faithful and hopeful, knowing that God is always true to His word, even when the wait feels long? _________

____

____

Today's affirmation: "I Am faithful to God while I wait."

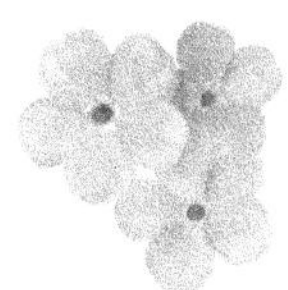

Prayer Prompt:

Faithful God, thank You for being a promise-keeper. Like Sarah, I sometimes grow weary in the waiting, but I want to trust You more deeply. Help me to stay faithful, hopeful, and patient as I wait for Your promises to unfold in my life. Strengthen my heart when doubts creep in, and remind me that Your timing is perfect. Today, I choose to trust You with...

____

____

____

____

____

____

____

 (Purple Rose – Represents transformation and dignity.)

"I Am" used by God despite my past, like Rahab. Joshua 2:1–21; Matthew 1:5 – Rahab in Jesus' lineage.

Rahab's story is one of hope, courage, and transformation. Rahab lived in the city of Jericho, a city that was about to face the Israelite army led by Joshua. Though she was known as a woman with a complicated past, often described as a prostitute, Rahab made a brave choice that changed her life forever.

When two Israelite spies came to Jericho, Rahab hid them from the king's soldiers, risking her safety. She believed in the God of Israel and understood that He was powerful and trustworthy. Rahab asked the spies to promise safety for her family when Israel came to take the city, and she helped them escape.

Because of her faith and courage, Rahab and her family were spared when Jericho was conquered. But her story doesn't end there. Rahab became part of Israel's community and was honored for her faith. In fact, she is listed in the genealogy of Jesus in Matthew 1:5, showing that God used her past for His greater purpose, to bring about the lineage of the Messiah.

Rahab's life teaches us that no past is too broken for God to redeem. When we trust Him, He can use our stories, no matter how complicated or difficult, to fulfill His promises and bless us and others.

When we say, "I am used by God despite my past, like Rahab," we claim that God's grace covers all, and He can make something beautiful from every life.

Do you truly believe that God can use you powerfully, no matter what's in your past? ____

What lies or labels that others have put on you, or you have put on yourself, that you need to release to fully embrace your identity and God's purpose for your life? ______________________________

____

____

____

Like Rahab, are you willing to take courageous steps of faith, even when they're risky or misunderstood, trusting that God is weaving your story into something greater than you can see?

____

____

____

Today's affirmation: "I Am used by God despite my past."

Prayer Prompt

Redeeming God, thank You for seeing beyond my past and calling me into purpose. Like Rahab, You have the power to transform my story and use it for Your glory. Remind me that my mistakes do not disqualify me, they are part of the testimony You're shaping. Help me to walk in bold faith, trusting that I am chosen and useful in Your hands. Help me sense and understand how you want to use me now. Today, I surrender my past and ask You to use me in...

____

____

____

____

____

____

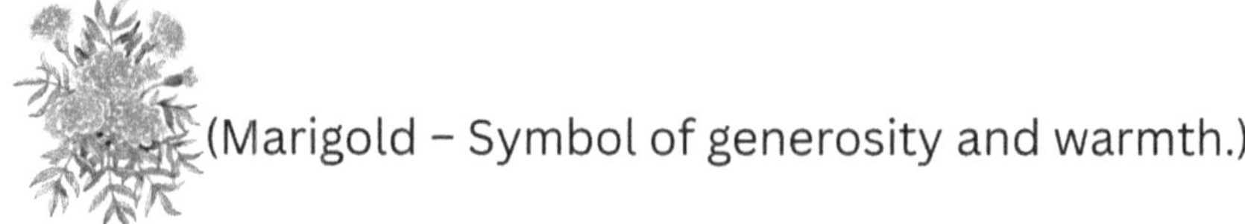(Marigold – Symbol of generosity and warmth.)

"I Am" generous and kind, like the Shunammite woman. 2 Kings 4:10 – She made room for God's prophet.

2 Kings 4:10 – "Let us make a small room on the roof and put a bed for him there, and a table and a chair and a lampstand, so that he can stay there whenever he comes to us."

The Shunammite woman was a kind and generous woman who showed great hospitality to the prophet Elisha. When Elisha traveled through her town, she noticed he was a holy man who brought God's presence and power wherever he went. Wanting to bless him, she and her husband made a special room for Elisha in their home, a quiet place where he could rest and feel welcome anytime he visited.

Her kindness went beyond just providing a room. She cared deeply for others and trusted God's power. When Elisha promised that she would have a son despite her old age, she believed and was later rewarded with the blessing of a child. Even when her son died, her faith did not waver, and through God's power, Elisha raised the boy back to life.

The Shunammite woman's story teaches us that generosity is not only about giving things, it is about opening our hearts and homes to others, especially those in need. Her kindness was a tangible way of showing God's love and hospitality.

When we say, "I am generous and kind, like the Shunammite woman," we commit to sharing what we have with others and trusting God to work through our acts of love.

Reflective Questions

In what ways are you making room in your life, your home, heart, and schedule for God's presence? _______________________________

____

In what ways are you making room in your life, your home, heart, and schedule for God's people? _______________________________

____

What might you need to release or rearrange to be more available to God? _______________________________

____

____

How can you show generosity and kindness today, not just out of abundance, but from a sincere desire to serve and honor God, like the Shunammite woman did?_______________________________

____

____

Today's affirmation: "I Am generous and kind."

Prayer Prompt

Lord, make my heart like the Shunammite woman's, open, generous, and willing to make room for You and those You send. Teach me to serve with kindness, not for recognition, but out of love and reverence for You. Show me how to use what I have, my home, my time, my resources, to be a blessing. Today, I ask You to help me be generous with...

____

____

____

____

____

____

(Gladiolus – Symbol of strength of character
and bold persistence.)

"I Am" bold in my prayers, like the Canaanite woman. Matthew 15:28 – "Woman, you have great faith!"

The Canaanite woman's story is a powerful example of boldness and persistence in prayer. When Jesus was traveling through the region of Tyre and Sidon, this woman came to Him, desperately seeking healing for her daughter who was suffering from a terrible illness. Though she was a Gentile and not part of the Jewish community, she did not hesitate to approach Jesus.

At first, Jesus seemed to ignore her and even said that His mission was primarily to the people of Israel. But the woman was not discouraged. She continued to humbly and boldly ask for His help, saying, "Lord, help me!" Her faith and persistence caught Jesus' attention.

Finally, Jesus praised her, saying, "Woman, you have great faith! Your request is granted." Because of her boldness in prayer and unwavering belief, her daughter was healed.

Her story teaches us that we can come to God boldly, with confidence and persistence, even when the answers don't come right away. Bold prayer is about trusting God's power and never giving up, no matter the obstacles.

When we say, "I am bold in my prayers, like the Canaanite woman," we claim the courage to approach God with faith and persistence, knowing that He listens and cares deeply.

Do you approach God with bold, persistent faith in prayer, believing He hears you even when answers seem delayed? _______

What is one area where you need to pray more boldly today?

How can you grow in a faith that refuses to give up, like the Canaanite woman, trusting God's heart even when His timing or response challenges your understanding? ______________

Today's affirmation: "I Am bold in my prayers."

Prayer Prompt:

Lord, I want to come to You with bold faith, believing that You hear me and respond with compassion and power. Like the Canaanite woman, help me to pray with persistence and confidence, even when answers feel delayed or uncertain. Strengthen my faith to keep seeking, keep asking, and keep trusting. Today, I come to You boldly and I pray for...

(Iris – Symbol of hope, renewal, and transformation.)

"I Am" redeemed and restored, like the woman at the well. John 4:29 – "Come, see a man who told me everything..."

John 4:29 – "Come, see a man who told me everything I ever did. Could this be the Messiah?"
The woman at the well was someone whose life had been marked by hardship and rejection. She had faced judgment from her community because of her past and her many relationships. When she met Jesus at the well, she expected to be seen as just another outcast.

Jesus surprised her. He spoke to her with kindness and revealed that He knew her entire life story, everything she had done. Instead of condemning her, Jesus offered her living water, a symbol of eternal life and renewal. He saw her not for her past mistakes, but for who she could become.

This encounter changed everything for the woman at the well. Filled with hope and joy, she ran back to her town, inviting others to "Come, see a man who told me everything I ever did. Could this be the Messiah?" She became one of the first to share the good news about Jesus, showing that God's love can redeem and restore anyone.

Her story reminds us that no one is beyond God's grace. When we say, "I am redeemed and restored, like the woman at the well," we declare that our past does not define us. God sees us, forgives us, and invites us into a new life filled with hope and purpose.

Reflective Questions

How has Jesus met you in a moment of brokenness or a hidden place? ____

____

What parts of your story is He redeeming and restoring for His glory? ____

____

Like the woman at the well, are you boldly sharing what Jesus has done in your life? ____________________________________
OR are you still hesitant? (Why?) ____________________________

____

____

What would it look like to testify freely and confidently about His transforming love? ____________________________________

____

____

Today's affirmation: "I Am redeemed and restored."

Prayer Prompt:

 Jesus, thank You for seeing me completely, and loving me anyway. Like the woman at the well, I bring You my past, my pain, and my need for healing. Thank You for meeting me in my brokenness and offering me living water that restores and renews. Help me to walk in the freedom of redemption and to boldly share what You've done in my life. Today, I lay before You...

____

____

____

____

____

YOU ARE DOING AN AWESOME JOB SIS. YOU ARE HALFWAY DONE

1. Journal entry #16 completed _______
2. Journal entry #17 completed _______
3. Journal entry #18completed _______
4. Journal entry #19 completed _______
5. Journal entry #20 completed _______
6. Journal entry #21 completed _______
7. Journal entry #22 completed _______
8. Journal entry #23 completed _______
9. Journal entry #24 completed _______
10. Journal entry #25 completed _______
11. Journal entry #26 completed _______
12. Journal entry #27 completed _______
13. Journal entry #28 completed _______
14. Journal entry #29 completed _______
15. Journal entry #30 completed _______

Are
you
Ready?
LET'S GO!

 (Pink Rose – Represents grace, forgiveness, and love.)

"I Am" forgiven and free, like the sinful woman with the alabaster jar.
Luke 7:47–48 – "Your sins are forgiven."

Luke 7:47–48 – "Therefore, I tell you, her many sins have been forgiven—as her great love has shown. But whoever has been forgiven little loves little." Then Jesus said to her, "Your sins are forgiven."

The sinful woman with the alabaster jar is a powerful example of forgiveness and love. This woman came to Jesus while He was dining at the house of a Pharisee named Simon.

She was known in her town for living a sinful life, and yet, she boldly approached Jesus with a jar of expensive perfume. She poured the fragrant oil over His feet, weeping and wiping them with her hair—an act of deep humility and love.

Many around her judged her harshly, but Jesus saw her heart. He recognized her great love and faith, which were born out of the forgiveness she had received. Jesus told her, "Your sins are forgiven," giving her freedom from guilt and shame.

Her story reminds us that no matter our past mistakes, God's forgiveness is available to all who come to Him with a repentant heart. Forgiveness brings freedom, and freedom leads to a love that overflows into acts of devotion and gratitude.

When we say, "I am forgiven and free, like the sinful woman with the alabaster jar," we claim the grace that washes away our sins and fills us with a love that honors Jesus.

Reflective Questions

Do you fully believe that you are forgiven and free, or are you still carrying guilt or shame from your past? _____________________
What would it look like for you to live each day in the freedom of God's grace? ____

____

____

Like the woman who poured out her worship in gratitude, how can you respond to God's forgiveness in a way that reflects deep love, humility, and surrender? _____________________________

____

____

Today's affirmation: "I Am forgiven and free."

Prayer Prompt

Jesus, thank You for the gift of forgiveness and the freedom that comes with it. Like the woman who poured out her love and tears at Your feet, I come with a grateful heart. I lay down my past, my guilt, and anything that holds me back from fully receiving Your grace. Help me to live each day in the freedom of Your love and to worship You with my whole heart. Today, I release...

____

____

____

____

____

____

____

"I Am" a worshiper in spirit and truth, like Mary of Bethany. John 12:3 – She anointed Jesus with perfume.

John 12:3 – "Then Mary took about a pint of pure nard, an expensive perfume; she poured it on Jesus' feet and wiped them with her hair. The house was filled with the fragrance of the perfume."

Mary of Bethany was a devoted follower of Jesus who demonstrated deep love and worship in a very personal and meaningful way. When Jesus visited her home, Mary took a costly jar of perfume and poured it over His feet, then wiped them with her hair, an act of great humility, honor, and devotion.

This was not just a simple act of kindness; it was a powerful expression of worship. Mary's heart was fully engaged as she honored Jesus with her time, her resources, and her presence. She worshiped Him in spirit, showing sincere love, and in truth, recognizing who He truly was.

Mary's worship was different from the busy distractions of others around her. She focused completely on Jesus, offering Him her best without hesitation or concern for what others might think. Her worship filled the room, leaving a lasting impression on everyone present.

Her story reminds us that true worship is more than rituals or words; it's about the condition of our hearts. When we say, "I am a worshiper in spirit and truth, like Mary of Bethany," we commit to honoring Jesus with genuine love, full attention, and sincere devotion.

Reflective Questions

Are you offering Jesus your most valuable "perfume," your time, talents, heart, or resources as an act of worship? ______________ Or are you holding something back? (Why?) __________________

____

What would wholehearted worship look like in your life today?

____

____

Do you worship God from a place of deep love and truth, like Mary, even when others may not understand or approve? ______

____

How can you grow in worship that is both intimate and bold?

____

____

Today's affirmation: "I Am a worshipper in spirit and truth."

Prayer Prompt

Lord, I want to worship You like Mary of Bethany—with a heart full of love, humility, and surrender. Teach me to bring You my very best, not out of duty, but from deep devotion. Help me to quiet the noise around me so I can focus on You, honoring You with my time, my gifts, and my life. Today, I pour out my heart in worship by...

____

____

____

____

____

____

____

 (Protea – Symbolizes strength, dignity, and uniqueness.)

"I Am" clothed with dignity and strength, like the Proverbs 31 woman. Proverbs 31:25 – "She is clothed with strength and dignity…"

Proverbs 31:25 – "She is clothed with strength and dignity; she can laugh at the days to come."

The Proverbs 31 woman is a powerful example of godly character, inner beauty, and purposeful living. She is not defined by her outward appearances or status, but by the strength of her spirit and the dignity with which she carries herself. Her strength comes from trusting in the Lord, and her dignity comes from knowing who she is in Him.

She is hardworking, wise, and compassionate. She manages her home with care, serves others with love, and speaks with wisdom and kindness. She doesn't fear the future because her faith gives her confidence; she can "laugh at the days to come," knowing that God is with her.

Although she wears many roles, wife, mother, businesswoman, leader, her identity is rooted in her relationship with God. She doesn't seek praise for herself, but her life naturally inspires respect and admiration.

The Proverbs 31 woman is not about being perfect; it's about living with purpose. She lives with intention, courage, and grace. Her life is a reflection of God's strength within her.

When we say, "I am clothed with dignity and strength, like the Proverbs 31 woman," we declare that we are empowered by God to live with confidence, honor, and purpose, no matter what season of our life we are in.

Reflective Questions

What does it truly mean for you to be "clothed with strength and dignity" in your daily life? ________________________________
____

How can you embrace the identity of being "clothed with strength and dignity" even in seasons of weakness or uncertainty? _______
____
____

In what ways can you reflect God's strength and dignity in how you carry yourself, speak to others, and respond to challenges that are both seen and unseen by others? _______________
____
____

Today's affirmation: "I Am clothed with dignity and strength."

Prayer Prompt

Lord, clothe me in Your strength and dignity today. When I feel weak, remind me that Your power is made perfect in my weakness. Help me walk with confidence, not in myself, but in who You say I am. Teach me to face the future without fear, trusting that You go before me. Today, I choose to stand strong in You by...

____
____
____
____
____
____

"I Am" trusted with the good news, like the women at the tomb. Matthew 28:7, "Go quickly and tell…"

Matthew 28:7 – "Then go quickly and tell his disciples: 'He has risen from the dead and is going ahead of you into Galilee.'" Early on the first Easter morning, a group of women went to Jesus' tomb with heavy hearts. Among them were Mary Magdalene and "the other Mary." They went to honor Jesus' body, expecting to find a sealed grave—but instead, they found an open tomb and an angel waiting with amazing news: "He is not here; He has risen!"

The angel then gave them a command: "Go quickly and tell…" These women were the very first to hear the news of Jesus' resurrection—and they were entrusted to share it with the disciples. In a time when women were often overlooked or underestimated, God chose them to carry the most important message the world would ever hear.

The women responded immediately. Filled with both fear and joy, they ran to tell the others. And as they went, they encountered Jesus Himself—alive and full of grace—confirming that the message they carried was true and powerful.

The story of the women at the tomb reminds us that God values willing hearts and faithful obedience. He chooses ordinary people—women, in this case—to carry out extraordinary tasks. Their trustworthiness and courage in that moment changed history.

When we say, "I am trusted with the good news, like the women at the tomb," we recognize that we, too, are called to share the message of hope, life, and resurrection with others— boldly, joyfully, and without delay.

Reflective Questions

Do you see yourself as someone God has entrusted with His truth? ____

In what ways are you boldly sharing the "good news" of Jesus with those around you–through your words, actions, or testimony?

____

____

____

What fears, doubts, or distractions may be holding you back from going "quickly" and obediently, like the women at the tomb? _____

____

How can you grow in courage and urgency to share God's message today? ____________________________________

____

____

Today's affirmation: "I Am trusted with good news."

Prayer Prompt

Lord, just as You chose the women at the tomb to be the first messengers of Your resurrection, You have also trusted me to carry the good news. Help me to move "quickly" to share your love, and not hold back because of fear or doubt. Who in my life needs to hear the hope and truth of Your Word today?

____

____

____

____

____

____

(Olive Blossom – A symbol of peace and reconciliation.)

"I Am" a peacemaker, like Abigail.
1 Samuel 25:18–35 – She calmed a dangerous conflict.

1 Samuel 25:18–35 – Abigail acted quickly… and brought peace where there could have been destruction. Abigail was a woman of wisdom, courage, and calm under pressure. Her story unfolds during a time of rising tension between David, who would later become king, and her husband Nabal, a harsh and foolish man. When David and his men requested kindness from Nabal, who had benefited from their protection, Nabal responded with insults and disrespect.

David, offended and angered, set out with his men, ready to take revenge. But Abigail, having heard what happened, quickly intervened. She gathered generous gifts, rode out to meet David, and humbly spoke words of peace and wisdom.

Abigail reminded David of his greater purpose and of God's promises for his future. Her calm, respectful, and courageous approach softened David's heart and stopped a violent conflict before it began. David praised her and said, "May you be blessed for your good judgment and for keeping me from bloodshed" (1 Samuel 25:33). Abigail's story shows us what it means to be a true peacemaker. She didn't ignore the problem or avoid confrontation; she faced it with wisdom, humility, and grace. She used her words and actions to protect others and honor God.

When we say, "I am a peacemaker, like Abigail," we commit to being agents of peace in our homes, communities, and relationships. Like Abigail, we can step into tense situations with calm strength and speak truth in love to bring about healing and restoration.

Reflective Questions

When faced with conflict, do you respond with wisdom and humility like Abigail, or do you react in ways that may escalate the situation? ____

What can you do to cultivate a heart that seeks peace first?

____

____

Is there a situation in your life where God is calling you to step in with calm words and a gentle spirit? _____________________________

____

How can you use your words, resources, or actions today to become an instrument of God's peace in your home, community, or relationships, just as Abigail courageously did? _____________

____

____

Today's affirmation: "I Am a peacemaker."

Father, make me a vessel of Your peace. Teach me to speak with grace, to act with discernment, and to carry Your calming presence into every room I enter. Use me to turn away anger and bring healing where it's needed most. Please help me not to react out of emotion, and respond with wisdom and humility. The situations and circumstances that I need help with my response is ...

____

____

____

____

____

____

____

 (Camellia – Represents perseverance and a courageous spirit.)

"I Am" persistent in faith, like the bleeding woman. Mark 5:28 – "If I just touch His clothes…"

Mark 5:28 – "If I just touch His clothes, I will be healed." The story of the bleeding woman is one of quiet desperation and remarkable faith. For twelve years, she suffered from a condition that left her physically weak, socially isolated, and spiritually discouraged. According to the laws of her time, her illness made her "unclean," forcing her to live on the fringes of society, unseen and untouched.

Doctors had no answers, and her resources were gone. Yet her faith remained. When she heard that Jesus was passing by, hope stirred within her. She didn't ask to speak to Him. She didn't demand attention. She simply believed, "If I just touch His clothes, I will be healed."

Pushing through the crowd, she reached out and touched the edge of His garment, and instantly, she was healed. Jesus noticed her touch and stopped. Rather than rebuking her, He honored her courage and said, "Daughter, your faith has healed you. Go in peace and be freed from your suffering." (Mark 5:34)

Her persistence in faith teaches us that even in our most desperate, invisible moments, Jesus sees us. Her story reminds us that faith is not always loud or public; it can be a silent reach in the middle of chaos, a determination to believe even when everything says it's hopeless.

When we say, "I am persistent in faith, like the bleeding woman," we claim the same determination to seek Jesus no matter the obstacles. We declare that our hope is in Him—and that even a single, faith-filled touch can change everything.

Reflective Questions

Are there situations in your life that feel hopeless or prolonged? _____ How can you hold onto faith like the bleeding woman, who believed that even the smallest step toward Jesus led to her healing? ____

____

____

Are you persistent in faith, like the bleeding woman? __________ Are you open to teaching and learning in partnership with others?

____

How can you embrace godly collaborations to help build the Kingdom of God more effectively? ____________________________

____

____

Today's affirmation: "I Am persistent in faith."

Prayer Prompt

Lord, help me to be like the woman in this story who didn't let fear, shame, or the crowd stop her. She believed healing was found in just one touch of You. Strengthen my faith when hope feels far away. Help me to keep reaching for You through the noise, the pain, the waiting, believing that even the smallest touch of Your presence can change everything. The things that I am pressing through today that are testing my faith are...

____

____

____

____

____

____

(Zinnia – Symbol of service, friendship, and lasting goodness.)

"I Am" a servant of the Lord, like Lydia. Acts 16:15 – "If you consider me a believer in the Lord…"

Acts 16:15 – "If you consider me a believer in the Lord… come and stay at my house." Lydia was a successful businesswoman from the city of Thyatira, known for selling purple cloth, a luxury item in the ancient world. She lived in Philippi, a Roman colony, and stood out not only for her work ethic and leadership but also for her devotion to God.

When Paul and his companions came to Philippi to share the message of Jesus, they found a group of women gathered for prayer by the river. Lydia was among them. As Paul spoke, the Lord opened Lydia's heart, and she believed. Immediately, she and her household were baptized. Her first response to her new faith was service: she invited Paul and his companions to stay in her home, offering hospitality and support to God's messengers.

Lydia's home soon became a center for the early church in Philippi. Her faith was not just private, it was active, generous, and impactful. She used her resources and influence to further God's kingdom.

Her life reminds us that being a servant of the Lord is not limited to a title or a role. It's a daily decision to welcome, to give, and to serve. Lydia's open heart led to an open home, and through her obedience, the gospel was planted in a new city.

When we say, "I am a servant of the Lord, like Lydia," we acknowledge our willingness to use our gifts, our homes, our work, and our lives to serve God and bless others.

How can you open your heart, and your home, time, or resources, to serve God and others like Lydia did with boldness and generosity? ____

____

____

Do you see your everyday work, relationships, and acts of kindness as part of your service to the Lord? ________________
How can you offer your everyday work, relationships, and acts of kindness more intentionally to God? ________________

____

____

Today's affirmation: "I Am a servant of the Lord."

Prayer Prompt:

Like Lydia, help me to open my heart, my home, and my hands for the sake of the gospel. Lord help me to make my faith more visible, so that it shows up in my actions, my hospitality, and service. Help me to make room for God and others in my everyday life. Lord, make me a woman who serves You with joy and boldness. Open my heart like Lydia's so I can see where You are at work, and join You there. Use my gifts, my home, and my life to bless others and glorify You. Help me to serve in the following areas...

____

____

____

____

____

____

 (Bay Laurel – Symbol of leadership, victory, and wisdom.)

"I Am" equipped to lead, like Priscilla.
Acts 18:26 – She taught Apollos with her husband.

Acts 18:26 – "When Priscilla and Aquila heard him, they invited him to their home and explained to him the way of God more accurately." Priscilla was a bold, intelligent, and spiritually grounded woman in the early church. Alongside her husband Aquila, she played a key role in spreading the gospel and strengthening the faith of others. The couple met the apostle Paul in Corinth, and their shared love for Christ and tentmaking turned into a powerful ministry partnership.

One of the most memorable moments in Priscilla's story occurs in Acts 18. A gifted speaker named Apollos arrived in Ephesus. He was passionate and knowledgeable about Scripture, but he didn't fully understand the message of Jesus.

Priscilla and Aquila noticed this and, rather than correcting him publicly, they wisely invited him into their home and lovingly taught him the truth more fully.

Priscilla didn't shy away from leadership or spiritual teaching. She used her knowledge, her faith, and her voice to lead with grace and clarity. Scripture consistently names her alongside her husband, sometimes even before him, highlighting her equal role in ministry.

Priscilla's example reminds us that leadership is not limited by gender, background, or title. It is rooted in our willingness to learn, serve, and boldly share what we know in love. She was not just a supporter of ministry, she was a leader in it.

When we say, "I am equipped to lead, like Priscilla," we affirm that God can use us to teach, guide, and impact others for His glory. Like Priscilla, we are called to lead with wisdom, humility, and a deep understanding of God's Word.

Reflective Questions

How are you using the spiritual wisdom and knowledge God has given you to teach, mentor, or encourage others in their faith, like Priscilla did with Apollos? _______________________________

____

Are you open to teaching and learning in partnership with others, and how can you embrace godly collaboration to help build the Kingdom of God more effectively? ______________________

____

____

Today's affirmation: "I Am equipped to lead."

Prayer Prompt

Lord, equip me to lead like Priscilla, in the areas that you have designed for me. Priscilla wasn't just present; she was prepared. She used her knowledge and voice to help someone grow in truth, leading with grace, wisdom, and humility. Help me to step up and lead, even if it feels unexpected. Lord, thank You for equipping me with truth, insight, and influence. Help me to lead with clarity and courage, like Priscilla. Teach me to speak Your Word with accuracy, walk in step with Your Spirit, and lead others closer to You, whether in quiet conversations or bold moments of teaching. The areas that I can serve as a leader are...____

____

____

____

____

"I Am" a helper to others, like Phoebe.
Romans 16:1–2 – A deacon and servant of the church...

Romans 16:1–2 – "I commend to you our sister Phoebe, a deacon of the church...She has been the benefactor of many people, including me."

Phoebe was a respected and trusted leader in the early church. The Apostle Paul speaks highly of her in his letter to the Romans, commending her to the believers and encouraging them to receive her with honor. He describes her as a servant (or deacon) of the church in Cenchreae and a benefactor—a person who generously helps and supports others.

Many scholars believe that Phoebe was the one who personally delivered Paul's letter to the Roman church. This was no small task. She not only carried the letter but likely explained its meaning to the believers there, acting as Paul's representative.

Phoebe's service was practical, spiritual, and deeply impactful. She gave of her time, her resources, and her leadership to strengthen the church and support those in ministry. Her example shows that helping others isn't a passive role, it's a powerful calling.

When we say, "I am a helper to others, like Phoebe," we declare that we are willing to serve with purpose, give generously, and support the work of God however He leads. Phoebe's legacy reminds us that quiet strength, faithful service, and a heart for others are vital to the growth of God's kingdom.

How are you currently using your time, resources, or influence to support and uplift others in your community, church, or family, like Phoebe did? ______________________________________

____

____

 How can you grow in seeing service as a form of worship and obedience to God? ______________________________________

____

____

Today's affirmation: "I Am a helper to others."

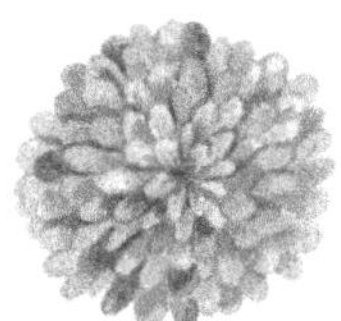

Prayer Prompt

God help me to be a helper to others, like Phoebe. Help me to faithfully serve my church and support others with generosity, strength, and humility. God help me to recognize those who are around me who need my support, encouragement, or practical help today.   Help me to serve with a willing heart. Lord, make me like Phoebe, steady, trusted, and ready to help. Show me how to serve without hesitation, give without holding back, and love without needing applause. Let my life be a reflection of Your servant heart. Those who may need me are....

____

____

____

____

____

____

 (Morning Glory – Opens with the morning and represents daily devotion.)

"I Am" devoted to prayer, like Anna the prophetess.
Luke 2:37 – "She never left the temple…"

Luke 2:37 – "She never left the temple but worshiped night and day, fasting and praying." Anna the prophetess appears only briefly in Scripture, but her devotion leaves a lasting impact. She was a widow, advanced in years, who spent her life in the temple, continually worshiping, fasting, and praying.

Her story is found in Luke 2, where she is among the first to recognize the infant Jesus as the promised Messiah. Despite the hardships she endured, including the loss of her husband after only seven years of marriage, Anna did not become bitter or withdrawn. Instead, she chose a life of devotion to God.

Her presence in the temple wasn't casual; it was consistent and purposeful. She worshiped with a heart full of faith and anticipation. When Mary and Joseph brought Jesus to the temple, Anna immediately gave thanks to God and began to speak about the child to all who were looking forward to the redemption of Jerusalem. Her prophetic voice and her constant intercession prepared the way for others to believe.

Anna reminds us that a life of prayer is powerful and purposeful. It may not always be seen by many, but it is always seen by God. Her quiet faithfulness helped usher in the message of Jesus' arrival.

When we say, "I am devoted to prayer, like Anna," we declare that we will stay spiritually alert, faithful in worship, and open to hearing God's voice. Anna's story encourages us that no matter our age, season, or status, our devotion makes a difference.

Reflective Questions

What distractions or habits might be keeping you from cultivating a deeper, more consistent prayer life? ____________________
____
____
How can you create space to meet with God daily like Anna did?
____
____
In what ways can you use prayer not just for personal needs, but as a way to intercede for others and stay spiritually connected to God's purpose in your life? _________________________________
____
What would change in your life if you prioritized prayer the way Anna did? ____
____

Today's affirmation: "I Am devoted to prayer."

Prayer Prompt

Dear God, help me to be devoted to prayer, like Anna the prophetess. Luke 2:37 – "She never left the temple but worshiped night and day, fasting and praying." Like Anna, I want to stay close to You, day and night, year after year. I don't want my devotion to be loud or flashy, but powerful, consistent, and heard by You. Help me to make space to be still and seek You, and not let prayer be just an afterthought in my busy day. God give me a heart like Anna, anchored in Your presence. Help me to carve out sacred time with You and to trust that You're moving even in the waiting. Let my devotion speak louder than my circumstances, and let prayer be the rhythm that shapes my life. God help me to place time in prayer with You in front of these areas in my life...
____
____
____

(Magnolia – A strong, showy flower
symbolizing dignity and value.)

"I Am" valuable in God's plan, like Miriam. Exodus 15:20–21 – Led Israel in worship.

Exodus 15:20–21 – "Then Miriam the prophet, Aaron's sister, took a timbrel (a tambourine) in her hand, and all the women followed her, with timbrels and dancing. Miriam sang to them: 'Sing to the Lord, for he is highly exalted…'"

Miriam, the sister of Moses and Aaron, played a significant role in the story of Israel's deliverance. As a young girl, she courageously watched over baby Moses when he was placed in a basket and floated down the Nile. She even spoke up to Pharaoh's daughter and helped reunite Moses with his mother, a bold and wise move that helped shape the future of God's people. Later, Miriam emerged as a leader in Israel, known as a prophetess and a powerful voice among the people.

After God parted the Red Sea and the Israelites crossed on dry land, it was Miriam who led the women in a joyful celebration of praise. With music and dancing, she worshiped God for His mighty deliverance. Her leadership shows that women are not only included in God's plan, but they are essential to it. Miriam's influence was spiritual, prophetic, and communal. She reminded the people to celebrate God's faithfulness and led them in giving Him the glory.

When we say, "I am valuable in God's plan, like Miriam," we affirm that our voice matters, our presence is needed, and our worship has power. Like Miriam, we can use our courage, leadership, and praise to encourage others and honor God.

How can you use your unique gifts, like Miriam used her voice and leadership, to point others to God and lead them in worship or encouragement? ____

____

____

Do you truly believe that your presence and role in God's plan matter? ________ If not, what truth from His Word do you need to embrace to change that belief? _____________________________

____

____

Today's affirmation: "I Am valuable in God's plan."

Prayer Prompt

Thank you, God, that I am valuable in Your plan, like Miriam. Father, help me to not only witness deliverance, but also to help lead others into praise. Help me to use my voice courageously to lift the eyes of people towards You. Help me to believe I have a role in Your bigger story. Help me to use my gifts, my voice, creativity, and influence to lead others closer to Him. God, thank You for creating me with purpose. Remind me that I am valuable in Your plan, not because of perfection, but because of Your calling. Like Miriam, teach me to lead with joy, sing with boldness, and help others see Your faithfulness through my life. The ways in which I can be valuable to You are...

____

____

____

____

____

____

 (Aster – A symbol of wisdom, guidance, and faith passed down.)

"I Am" an example of faith to others, like Lois and Eunice. 2 Timothy 1:5 – Their faith lived on in Timothy.

2 Timothy 1:5 – "I am reminded of your sincere faith, which first lived in your grandmother Lois and in your mother Eunice…" Lois and Eunice are shining examples of generational faithfulness. In the New Testament, the apostle Paul commends Timothy's heartfelt and sincere faith by highlighting the influence of his grandmother Lois and his mother Eunice.

Their unwavering trust in God wasn't a private matter; it was so powerful and genuine that it shaped an entire life and became a legacy passed down to future generations. Both Lois and Eunice exemplified what it means to live a life steeped in faith.

Their commitment to God was not only seen in their actions but also demonstrated through the nurturing of Timothy's spiritual journey. This legacy reminds us that the examples set by those who come before us can inspire and guide our walk with God. Their lives teach us that everyday acts of faith, prayer, worship, Scripture study, and loving service can create ripples that extend far beyond one's lifetime. Just as Timothy's faith was enriched and sustained by his grandmother and mother, so too can our lives influence others.

When we say, "I am an example of faith to others, like Lois and Eunice," we commit to living a life that not only honors God in the present but also leaves a lasting impact on those who follow. Lois and Eunice encourage us to invest in relationships, to nurture faith in our families and communities, and to be consistent in our spiritual journey. Their legacy is a powerful reminder that our faithful example matters, and it can inspire someone today to live a life of trust in God.

Reflective Questions

What kind of faith legacy are you leaving for the people around you, especially the next generation? ___________________

____

____

What do you want that legacy to look like? ___________________

____

Who has seen your faith in action lately? ___________________

____

How can you continue to be a living example of God's love, strength, and truth in everyday moments? ___________________

____

____

Today's affirmation: "I Am an example of faith to others."

Prayer Prompt

Lord help me to be an example of faith to others, like Lois and Eunice (2 Timothy 1:5 – "I am reminded of your sincere faith, which first lived in your grandmother Lois and in your mother Eunice...") . Help me not to just talk about faith, but live it, and create a legacy that will help shape those that I come in contact with. Help me to display a quiet, consistent example that plants seeds that will bear fruit for generations. Let my faith be something others can see, not just in words, but in how I live. Help me to recognize who is watching me so that I may be an influence, even when I am unaware. Lord, help me to live a faith that's real, rooted, and contagious. May my life quietly echo Your truth, just like Lois and Eunice. Use me to pass on a legacy of faith, not through perfection, but through persistence, love, and trust in You.

____

____

____

 (Freesia – Symbol of trust and obedience.)

"I Am" obedient to God's voice, like Rebekah.
Genesis 24:58 – "I will go."

Genesis 24:58 – "They said to Rebekah, 'Will you go with this man?' 'I will go,' she said." Rebekah's story is a beautiful example of trusting and obeying God's guidance, even when the path is uncertain.

When Abraham's servant was sent to find a wife for Isaac, he prayed for God's direction and then met Rebekah at a well. After hearing the servant's story and God's plan, Rebekah was faced with a big decision: to leave her family and homeland to marry a man she had never met.

Without hesitation, Rebekah responded, "I will go." Her willingness to obey showed great faith and courage. She trusted that God's voice was leading her to something good, even though it meant stepping into the unknown.

Her obedience led to blessings not only for her but for the entire nation of Israel. Rebekah became the mother of twins, Esau and Jacob, and played a vital role in God's unfolding plan.

Rebekah's example reminds us that obedience often requires courage and trust. When we say, "I am obedient to God's voice, like Rebekah," we commit to listening carefully to God's direction and responding with faith, even when the future feels uncertain.

Her story encourages us that God's plans are always worth following, and that obedience opens the door for His blessings in our lives.

Reflective Questions

When was the last time you clearly sensed God leading you in a direction that felt unfamiliar or uncertain? __________________

____

When you felt led by God, did you respond with trust like Rebekah, or did you hesitate? ______________________________

____

____

What might you be holding onto that's keeping you from fully saying, "I will go" to God? ______________________________

____

If you are holding on to something, how can you surrender it today? ____

____

Today's affirmation: "I Am obedient to God's voice."

Prayer Prompt

Lord, I want to be obedient to God's voice, like Rebekah. Genesis 24:58 – "Then they called Rebekah and asked her, 'Will you go with this man?' And she said, 'I will go.'" Lord, when you direct me, I pray that I will not delay or debate, but that I will say yes in faith, trusting Your plan for my future. May my obedience help to open doors to Your greater purpose. I pray that when You call me out of the familiar, that I will be willing to say, "I will go." Help me to hear and know Your voice. I pray for comfort, as I trust You, not allow fear to hinder me, and walk in obedience for the path that You have for me. Give me comfort, even when the complete path isn't fully clear to me. I say "yes" to Your voice, knowing You go before me, un these areas of my life...

____

____

____

"I Am" blessed among women, like Mary, the mother of Jesus. Luke 1:42 – "Blessed are you among women…"

Luke 1:42 – "Blessed are you among women, and blessed is the child you will bear!" Mary, the mother of Jesus, holds a special place in the Bible and in the hearts of believers because of her faithful response to God's extraordinary call.

Mary was a young woman from Nazareth, chosen to carry the Son of God into the world, a task that came with great responsibility, potential shame, and risk. Despite her fear and uncertainty, Mary humbly submitted to God's will, saying, "I am the Lord's servant." When Mary visited her relative Elizabeth, who was also miraculously expecting a child, Elizabeth was filled with the Holy Spirit and exclaimed, "Blessed are you among women!" This declaration honored Mary's unique role in God's redemptive plan and recognized her faith-filled heart.

Mary was not just blessed because she became the mother of Jesus; she was blessed because she believed God's promises. Her life reminds us that true blessing is not about status or comfort, but about being chosen by God and trusting Him completely.

When we say, "I am blessed among women, like Mary," we declare that we, too, are seen, chosen, and deeply loved by God. We are blessed when we respond to His calling with faith and surrender, no matter how big or small our assignment may seem. Mary's life encourages every woman to walk boldly in her calling, knowing that God honors a willing heart.

Reflective Questions

How can you embrace God's calling on your life with the same faith and humility that Mary showed, even when you don't fully understand His plan? ______________________________________

____

____

In what ways has God already shown you His favor and blessings?

____

____

____

____

How can you respond to God's favor and blessings with gratitude and boldness like Mary? ______________________________________

____

____

Today's affirmation: "I Am blessed among women."

Prayer Prompt

Take time to reflect on Mary's unique blessing and her humble acceptance of God's plan.

Dear God, help me to recognize the blessings in my life, and to walk with the same grace and faith that Mary showed. Help me to feel honored and set apart in my journey through life, knowing that I am blessed among women in God's eyes. The areas in my life that I want God's blessings are...

____

____

____

____

____

(Cherry Blossom – Represents beauty, uniqueness, and the miracle of life.)

"I Am" fearfully and wonderfully made – A truth for all women. Psalm 139:14 – "I praise you because I am fearfully and wonderfully made..."

Psalm 139:14 – "I praise you because I am fearfully and wonderfully made; your works are wonderful, I know that full well." From Genesis to Revelation, the Bible introduces us to women of courage, wisdom, love, and unwavering faith.

Though their stories span centuries, one truth ties them all together: they were fearfully and wonderfully made by God, each created with purpose, strength, and dignity. Sarah believed in God's promise even after years of waiting. Esther risked her life to save her people. Deborah led Israel as both judge and prophet. Ruth left everything behind to stay loyal to her mother-in-law and ultimately became part of Jesus' lineage.

Hannah prayed earnestly and gave her son to God's service. Mary, the mother of Jesus, said "yes" to God's plan even when it was hard to understand. And women like Priscilla, Lydia, Anna, and Phoebe carried the gospel forward in the early church with courage and faith. None of these women was perfect; they were all purposely designed by a perfect Creator.

Psalm 139:14 reminds us that our worth isn't based on outward achievements or appearance—it's rooted in the fact that we were made by God Himself, with thought, care, and intention. When we declare, "I am fearfully and wonderfully made," we affirm that God created each woman with beauty, strength, and divine purpose. Like the faithful women of the Bible, we are invited to live lives that reflect God's love, walk in His truth, and trust His plan, because we are His marvelous creation.

Reflective Questions

In what areas of your life have you struggled to believe that you are wonderfully made? ____

____

How can you begin to see yourself through God's eyes instead of through your insecurities? ___________________________________

____

____

How does knowing that you are fearfully and wonderfully made change the way you speak to yourself, treat your body, and show up in relationships with others? ________________________________

____

____

Today's affirmation: "I Am fearfully and wonderfully made."

Prayer Prompt

Take a moment to quiet your heart...

Thank you, God, for the unique way You created me. The truth is that I am fearfully and wonderfully made, exactly as YOU intended. Help me to see myself through Your eyes, embracing my worth and beauty, not by the world's standards, but by YOUR perfect design. Give me confidence to walk boldly in the identity You have given me, knowing I am deeply loved and valued.

____

____

____

____

____

Congratulations!

You did it!

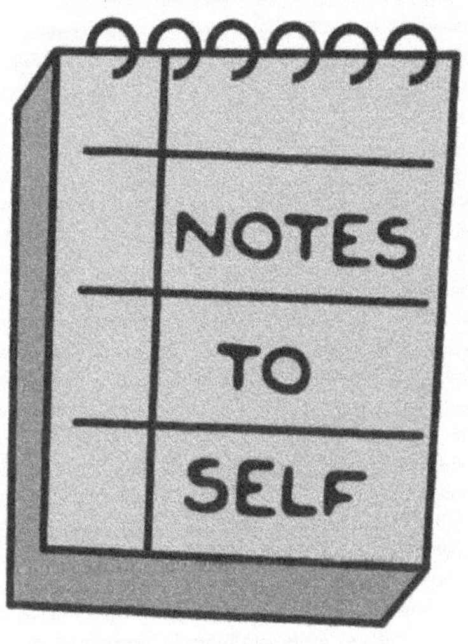

NOTES
TO
SELF

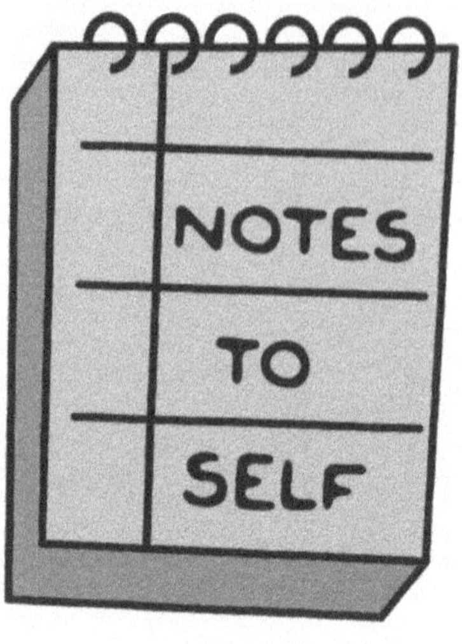
NOTES
TO
SELF

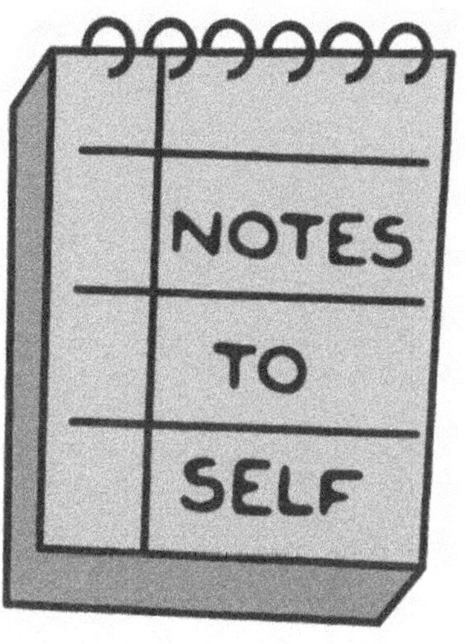
NOTES
TO
SELF

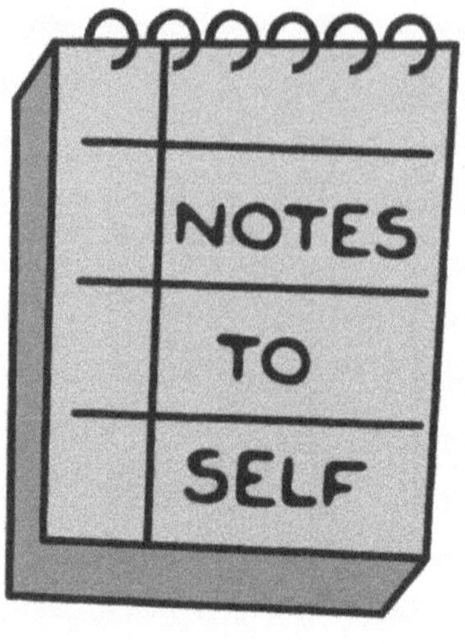

NOTES
TO
SELF

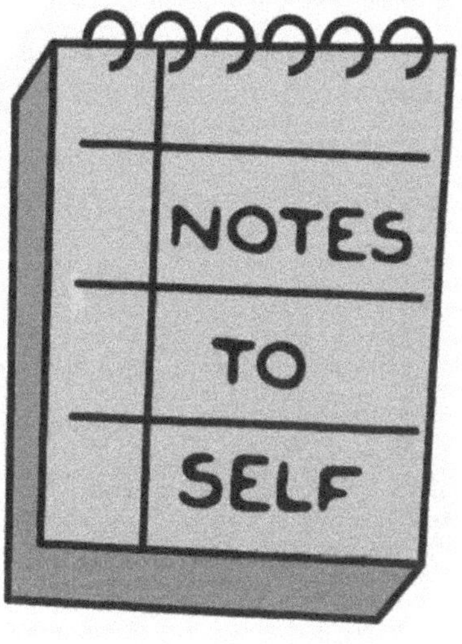

NOTES
TO
SELF

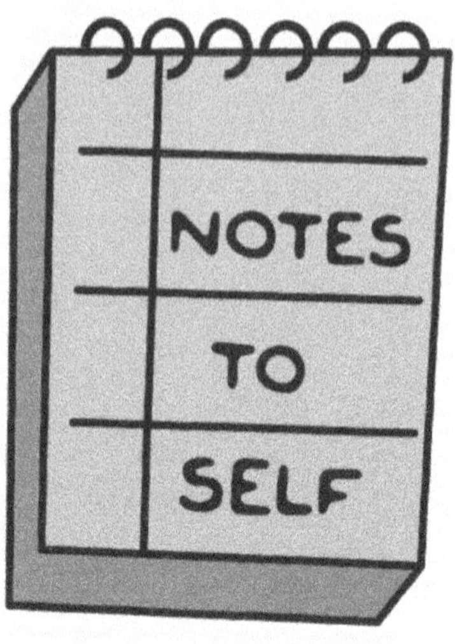
NOTES
TO
SELF

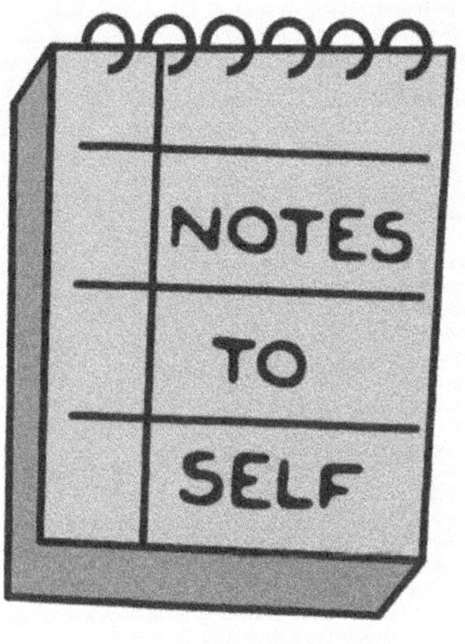

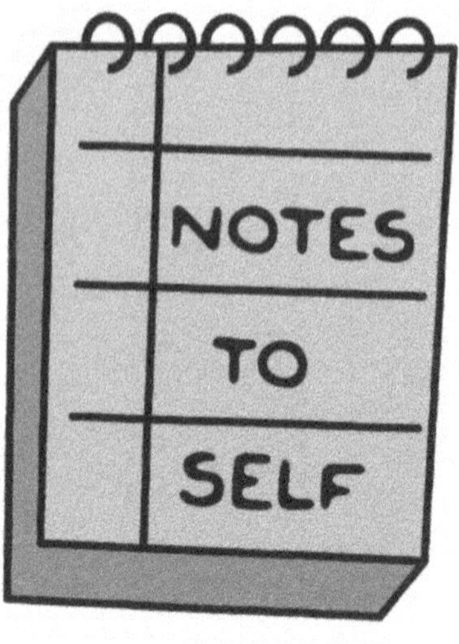

NOTES
TO
SELF

www.ingramcontent.com/pod-product-compliance
Lightning Source LLC
Chambersburg PA
CBHW050014040726
47599CB00014B/1368